CONNECT BIBLE STUDIES

The Matrix

Andy & Larry Wachowski
(Warner, 1999)

Reality and Truth
Technology
Freedom
Faith

www.connectbiblestudies.com

connect

linking the Word to the world

CONNECT BIBLE STUDIES: The Matrix

Published in this format by Scripture Union, 207-209 Queensway, Bletchley, MK2 2EB, England.

Scripture Union is a charitable organisation working around the world with the goal of making God's good news known to people of all ages and encouraging them to meet God regularly through the Bible and prayer. As well as publishing books, Bible reading notes, and a range of church resources, SU produces videos and audio cassettes, works in schools, and runs holidays, clubs and missions for children and young people.

Email: info@scriptureunion.org.uk
Internet: www.scriptureunion.org.uk

© Damaris Trust, PO Box 200, Southampton, SO17 2DL.

Damaris Trust enables people to relate Christian faith and contemporary culture. It helps them to think about the issues within society from a Christian perspective and to explore God's truth as it is revealed in the Bible. Damaris provides resources via the Internet, workshops, publications and products.

Email: office@damaris.org
Internet: www.damaris.org

ALSO AVAILABLE AS AN ELECTRONIC DOWNLOAD: www.connectbiblestudies.com

Chief editor: Nick Pollard
Consultant Editor: Andrew Clark
Managing Editor: Di Archer
Written by Di Archer, Caroline Puntis, Tony Watkins

First published 2001
ISBN 1 85999 579 9

British Library Cataloguing-in-Publication Data: a catalogue record for this book is available from the British Library.

Cover design and print production by:
CPO, Garcia Estate, Canterbury Road, Worthing, West Sussex BN13 1BW.

Other titles in this series:

Harry Potter and the Goblet of Fire ISBN 1 85999 578 0
U2: All That You Can't Leave Behind ISBN 1 85999 580 2
Billy Elliot ISBN 1 85999 581 0

And more titles following — check www.connectbiblestudies.com for latest titles or ask at any good Christian bookshop.

connect
linking the Word to the world

Using Connect Bible Studies

What Are These Studies?

These innovative home group Bible studies have two aims. Firstly, we design them to enable group members to dig into their Bibles and get to know them better. Secondly, we aim to help members to think through topical issues in a Biblical way. Hence the studies are based on a current popular book or film etc. The issues raised by these are the subjects for the Bible studies.

We do not envisage that all members will always be able to watch the films or read the books, or indeed that they will always want to. A summary is always provided. However, our vision is that knowing about these films and books empowers Christians to engage with friends and colleagues about them. Addressing issues from a Biblical perspective gives Christians confidence that they know what they think, and can bring a distinctive angle to bear in conversations.

The studies are produced in sets of four — i.e. four weeks' worth of group Bible Study material. These are available in print published by Scripture Union from your local Christian bookshop, or via the Internet at www.connectbiblestudies.com. Anyone can sign up for a free monthly email newsletter that announces the new studies and provides other information (sign up on the Connect Bible Studies website at www.connectbiblestudies.com/uk/register).

How Do I Use Them?

We design the studies to stimulate creative thought and discussion within a Biblical context. Each section therefore has a range of questions or options from which you as leader may choose in order to tailor the study to your group's needs and desires. Different approaches may appeal at different times, so the studies aim to supply lots of choice. Whilst adhering to the main aim of corporate Bible study, some types of questions may enable this for your group better than others — so take your pick.

Group members should be supplied with the appropriate sheet that they can fill in, each one also showing the relevant summary.

Leader's notes contain:

1.   Opening Questions

These help your group settle in to discussion, whilst introducing the topics. They may be straightforward, personal or creative, but are aiming to provoke a response.

2.   Summary

We suggest the summary of the book or film will follow now, read aloud if necessary. There may well be reactions that group members want to express even before getting on to the week's issue.

3.   Key Issue

Again, either read from the leader's notes, or summarised.

4.   Bible Study

Lots of choice here. Choose as appropriate to suit your group — get digging into the Bible. Background reading and texts for further help and study are suggested, but please use the material provided to inspire your group to explore their Bibles as much as possible. A concordance might be a handy standby for looking things up. A commentary could be useful too. The idea is to help people to engage with the truth of God's word, wrestling with it if necessary but making it their own.

Don't plan to work through every question here. Within each section the two questions explore roughly the same ground but from different angles or in different ways. Our advice is to take one question from each section. The questions are open-ended so each ought to yield good discussion — though of course any discussion in a Bible study may need prompting to go a little further.

5.   Implications

Here the aim is to tie together the perspectives gained through Bible study and the impact of the book or film. The implications may be personal, a change in worldview, or new ideas for relating to non-churchgoers. Choose questions that adapt to the flow of the discussion.

6.   Prayer

Leave time for it! We suggest a time of open prayer, or praying in pairs if the group would prefer. Encourage your members to focus on issues from your study that had a particular impact on them. Try different approaches to prayer — light a candle, say a prayer each, write prayers down, play quiet worship music — aim to facilitate everyone to relate to God.

7.   Background Reading

You will find links to some background reading on the Connect Bible Studies website: www.connectbiblestudies.com/

8.   Online Discussion

You can discuss the studies online with others on the Connect Bible Studies website at www.connectbiblestudies.com/discuss/

linking the Word to the world

The Matrix

Andy & Larry Wachowski
(Warner, 1999)

Part One: Reality & Truth

You ever have that feeling where you're not sure if you're awake or still dreaming? (Morpheus)

Please read Using Connect Bible Studies *before leading a Bible study using this material.*

Opening Questions

Choose one of these questions.

How do we know what is real?	Put a spoon in a glass of water. Does the spoon bend? How do you know?
In the film, would you have chosen the red pill or the blue pill? Why?	If solid matter actually consists of millions of atoms, is it real?

Summary

Thomas Anderson works in a grey office by day and becomes the troubled computer hacker 'Neo' by night. One night he wakes to find an intriguing message on his computer screen. It leads him to a woman called Trinity who used to be a hacker as well: 'I know why you're here, Neo ... I know because I was once looking for the same thing ... It's the question that drives us, Neo ... You know the question, just as I did ...' He replies without hesitating, 'What is the Matrix?'

Trinity takes Neo to meet Morpheus, who explains that, 'Unfortunately, no one can be told what the Matrix is. You have to see it for yourself.' He offers Neo a choice of two pills — if he takes the blue pill, Neo will carry on his life as before; if he takes the red pill, the truth of the Matrix will be revealed to him.

Neo takes the red pill. Reality warps — he touches a mirror and its silvery substance flows onto his fingers and engulfs his entire body. Neo's world recedes, revealing a horrifying and unbelievable truth — he is cocooned in a pod along with billions of other people whose brains are all connected to a computer program called the Matrix. It was designed to fool humans into believing that they exist in the world as it was in 1999. The year is in fact nearer 2099 and the world is run by machines powered by human energy.

Key Issues: Reality and Truth

Christians have been accused of pushing Christian interpretations of The Matrix too far. However, the symbolism is impossible to ignore — from names such as Trinity and Thomas, to concepts like Zion, truth, freedom etc. When questioned, the Wachowski brothers acknowledged that the references were intentional, but not limited to Christian perspectives. The Matrix is itself a perception of reality that is not the whole truth. Christians would argue also for a worldview that takes into account realms beyond that which we see, smell and touch. What is real? What is the truth of reality beyond our immediate experience? How do we know what is true, or how do we find it? How does it affect everyday life?

Bible Study

Choose one question from each section.

1. **What is real?**

   What is real? How do you define real? If you're talking about what you can feel, what you can smell, what you can taste and see, then 'real' is just electrical signals interpreted by your brain. (Morpheus)

   Leaders: The Matrix is picking up on an increasingly common idea that what we think of as the real world is simply an illusion, something in our brains. This section is primarily intended to affirm the reality of the physical world.

   ◆ Read Genesis 1:1–10, 26–31. What does the Bible see as real? What difference does it make?

      *Leaders: The point of this question is to explore the **fact** of creation — do not get sidetracked into discussions over creation and evolution. It is important to acknowledge that Christians have a range of opinion over this subject but **all** are agreed that God is the creator.*

   ◆ Read Acts 17:24–28. Describe in your own words the relationship between God and his creation.

      Leaders: see also Colossians 1:15–17; Hebrews 1:1–3a.

2. **A reality beyond our immediate experience**

   Have you felt that there is something wrong with the world — like a splinter in your mind driving you mad? 'IT' is everywhere ... all around us — even now. It is the world that has been pulled over your eyes to blind you to the truth. (Morpheus)

   Leaders: This section is primarily intended to affirm the reality of the spiritual world.

- ◆ Read 2 Corinthians 4:1–6, 16–18. In what ways has the 'god of this age' blinded the minds of unbelievers? What does Paul see as the Christian's response to this situation?

    Leaders: See also Colossians 3:1–4.

- ◆ For many years the West has been dominated by a view of life that sees only physical things as being real. Read Colossians 1:15–20. Why is it so hard for people to believe in spiritual things? What has this done to our own thinking about the spiritual world?

    Leaders: see also Ephesians 6:10–18.

3. The search for truth

The answer is looking for you; it will find you if you want it to. (Morpheus)

Leaders: Neo was searching for Morpheus but Morpheus was in fact already helping Neo to find him. In John 14:6 Jesus makes it clear that he IS the truth. Any search for truth will only find its fulfilment when it leads to Jesus Christ.

- ◆ Read 2 Chronicles 15:1–15. What did it mean for these people to seek God? Why was it such a serious business that dissenters were to be put to death (v. 13)?

    Leaders: 'Those who would not seek the Lord' (v. 13) would have been those who were determined to continue with worshipping false gods. This was a time for the whole nation to re-establish their purity and wholehearted commitment to God (especially in contrast to the northern kingdom which had introduced calf-worship at Dan and Bethel).

- ◆ Read Luke 19:1–10. What is involved in searching for truth? Put yourself in the place of Zacchaeus. Would you have been so determined to see Jesus if you had known the cost it would entail?

4. Living the truth or living a lie

For the longest time I wouldn't believe it and then I saw the fields with my own eyes ... And standing there, facing the pure horrifying precision, I came to realise the obviousness of the truth. (Morpheus)

Leaders: Try to help your group to understand that truth is something to be lived, not merely a set of facts.

- ◆ 1 John 1:5–2:11. Why does John use the metaphor of light for truth? How do we know when we are living in the truth?

- ◆ Read Psalm 119:25–48. What does it mean to choose the 'way of truth'? How do we do so?

Implications

I didn't say it would be easy, Neo. I just said it would be the truth. (Morpheus)

Choose one or more of the following questions.

♦ How does knowing the truth about the reality of the world affect the way we live?

♦ How would you answer someone who thinks life is an illusion?

♦ Does finding Jesus mean you have stopped searching?

♦ Those who would not seek God in 2 Chronicles 15 were to be put to death. What of those who refuse today? How can you inspire others to search for the truth?

♦ Use Psalm 104 as a meditation on creation. Read it aloud to quiet music, and enjoy the truth of all God has provided.

Prayer

Spend some time praying through these issues.

Background Reading

You will find links to some background reading on the Connect Bible Studies website: www.connectbiblestudies.com/uk/catalogue/0002/background.htm

Discuss

Discuss this study in the online discussion forums at www.connectbiblestudies.com/discuss

Members' sheet: The Matrix — Part 1

Summary

Thomas Anderson works in a grey office by day and becomes the troubled computer hacker 'Neo' by night. One night he wakes to find an intriguing message on his computer screen. It leads him to a woman called Trinity who used to be a hacker as well: 'I know why you're here, Neo ... I know because I was once looking for the same thing ... It's the question that drives us, Neo ... You know the question, just as I did ...' He replies without hesitating, 'What is the Matrix?'

Trinity takes Neo to meet Morpheus, who explains that, 'Unfortunately, no one can be told what the Matrix is. You have to see it for yourself.' He offers Neo a choice of two pills — if he takes the blue pill, Neo will carry on his life as before; if he takes the red pill, the truth of the Matrix will be revealed to him.

Neo takes the red pill. Reality warps — he touches a mirror and its silvery substance flows onto his fingers and engulfs his entire body. Neo's world recedes, revealing a horrifying and unbelievable truth — he is cocooned in a pod along with billions of other people whose brains are all connected to a computer program called the Matrix. It was designed to fool humans into believing that they exist in the world as it was in 1999. The year is in fact nearer 2099 and the world is run by machines powered by human energy.

Key Issue

Bible Study notes

Implications

Prayer

www.connectbiblestudies.com

connect
linking the Word to the world

The Matrix

Andy & Larry Wachowski
(Warner, 1999)

Part Two: Technology

***We marvelled at our own magnificence
as we gave birth to A.I. [Artificial Intelligence].*** (Morpheus)

Please read Using Connect Bible Studies *before leading a Bible study using this material.*

Opening Questions

Choose one of these questions.

What piece of technology do you regard as essential to your life?	What aspects of technology do you really dislike? Why?
Has technology improved your ability to communicate with others?	What technology would you like to invent to make the world a better place?

Summary

The world Neo had known was not real — it had been taken over by artificial intelligence machines. Humans are now only kept alive as the machines' sole source of energy. They lie cocooned in an array of individual pods having their energy drained off. Their brains are connected to a computer simulation called the Matrix. The Matrix deceives their brains into thinking that they live in something like the world at the end of the twentieth century. Neo's 'reality' is an illusion.

Morpheus and his crew of rebels live on a hovercraft ship in a network of underground sewers and rely on technology to survive. They locate the pod containing Neo's body and free him from it. Morpheus initiates Neo into their bleak world by means of a computer program that simulates the Matrix. A plug inserted into the back of his head connects his brain to a computer system. One of the crew downloads training programs into Neo's brain — he learns martial arts in a matter of seconds. The rebels can also plug into the Matrix from their ship, which means that they can interact with the enemy Agent programs created by the machines to destroy them. If they get killed in the Matrix they die in reality, since the body cannot live without the mind. The rebels' only weapon against the machines is an electro-magnetic pulse that disables all electrical systems in the vicinity.

Key Issue: Technology

Technology is practically impossible to escape in the Western world. The Matrix develops this to the extent that everyone's survival is totally dependent on technology. No life is possible without the use of machines. It could be argued that technology is heading that way for us too. Its advance seems rampant, with no time to catch our breath and consider the ethical and future implications. It inspires various reactions among people, from fear to excitement, from worry to enthusiasm for its potential. Jesus may not have driven a car, or worn a suit, but can the Bible still inform our attitudes towards the technology that increasingly dominates our lives? Are there principles to discern that can help us respond to our technological world with integrity and understanding?

Bible Study

Choose one question from each section.

1.   Technology in the beginning

When the Matrix was first built there was a man born inside who had the ability to change whatever he wanted, to remake the Matrix as he saw fit. It was he who freed the first of us, taught us the truth. (Morpheus)

Leaders: God's intention is for us to subdue and care for the earth. What he made was good. Technology is an expression of creativity but frequently emphasises subduing over care.

◆   Read Genesis 1:26–28; 2:4–20. How did God originally intend us to relate to creation? In what way has the Fall affected this?

   Leaders: The Fall has affected the productivity of the land. Caring for it is hard work.

◆   Read Genesis 4:17–22. Cain and Tubal-Cain are building cities and making tools. Were these the first beginnings of technology? Were they caring for creation and/or subduing it?

2.   Misuse of technology

We marvelled at our own magnificence as we gave birth to A.I. (Morpheus)

◆   Read Genesis 11:1–9. What were men aiming at in building the tower? What was wrong with that — why was it offensive to God?

   Leaders: Technological advances tend to be seen as a mark of human progress. But if they are an attempt to gain ultimate control over human destiny, they can deny God.

◆   Read Isaiah 31:1–3. What was Isaiah chastising his contemporaries for? Was the contemporary technology (i.e. horses pulling chariots) wrong in itself?

3. Good attitudes towards technology

Neo: *What are you trying to tell me — that I can dodge bullets?*

Morpheus: **No Neo, I'm trying to tell you that when you're ready, you won't have to.**

Leaders: Agent Smith thinks he can defeat Neo because his powers are superior. But Neo wins because he comes to believe he is the 'chosen one'. Our belief in God must be the determining factor in all our attitudes.

♦ Read I Samuel 17:4–11, 38–50. God was on David's side because David was on God's. What advantages did Goliath apparently have? Why did David win? What does this imply for our attitudes to technology and other material advantages we may have?

♦ Read Micah 4:1–5. What is the motivation for turning weapons to peaceful use? Can we achieve this without reference to God?

4. Living in a technological world

The Matrix is a system, Neo. That system is our enemy. And when you're inside you look around and what do you see? Businessmen, teachers, lawyers, carpenters — the very minds of the people we are trying to save. (Morpheus)

Leaders: Neo had to choose to deal with the world as he found it.

♦ Read 1 Timothy 6:17–19. How does this passage help us to have a right attitude towards technological wealth?

♦ Matthew 9:9–13. Neo and friends cared about their deceived contemporaries. They kept going back into their world. How did Jesus embrace the world he was part of?

Implications

What is the Matrix? Control. The Matrix is a computer-generated dream world, built to keep us under control in order to change a human being into — this. (Morpheus, holding up a battery).

Choose one or more of the following questions.

♦ In The Matrix technology is used to deceive, suppress and dehumanise. Is this necessarily the case in our world? Can we do anything about it?

♦ The technology industry is largely driven by consumer demand. Are there reasons to limit our consumption? How?

♦ How can you use technological products to further the cause of the kingdom?

♦ If the Matrix technology is both fascinating and frightening, what would you say to a friend who fears it could really happen?

Prayer

Spend some time praying through these issues.

Background Reading

You will find links to some background reading on the Connect Bible Studies website: www.connectbiblestudies.com/uk/catalogue/0002/background.htm

Discuss

Discuss this study in the online discussion forums at www.connectbiblestudies.com/discuss

Members' sheet: The Matrix — Part 2

Summary

The world Neo had known was not real — it had been taken over by artificial intelligence machines. Humans are now only kept alive as the machines' sole source of energy. They lie cocooned in an array of individual pods having their energy drained off. Their brains are connected to a computer simulation called the Matrix. The Matrix deceives their brains into thinking that they live in something like the world at the end of the twentieth century. Neo's 'reality' is an illusion.

Morpheus and his crew of rebels live on a hovercraft ship in a network of underground sewers and rely on technology to survive. They locate the pod containing Neo's body and free him from it. Morpheus initiates Neo into their bleak world by means of a computer program that simulates the Matrix. A plug inserted into the back of his head connects his brain to a computer system. One of the crew downloads training programs into Neo's brain — he learns martial arts in a matter of seconds. The rebels can also plug into the Matrix from their ship, which means that they can interact with the enemy Agent programs created by the machines to destroy them. If they get killed in the Matrix they die in reality, since the body cannot live without the mind. The rebels' only weapon against the machines is an electro-magnetic pulse that disables all electrical systems in the vicinity.

Key Issue

Bible Study notes

Implications

Prayer

linking the Word to the world

The Matrix

Andy & Larry Wachowski
(Warner, 1999)

Part Three: Freedom

As long as the Matrix exists, the human race will never be free.
(Morpheus)

Please read Using Connect Bible Studies *before leading a Bible study using this material.*

Opening Questions

Choose one of these questions.

Why do we want to be free?	If you painted a picture of freedom, what colours would you use?
Can freedom ever be a bad thing? Why?	What part of the world would you most like to set free?

Summary

Morpheus is captain of the Nebuchadnezzar, a hovercraft crewed by rebels who have been freed from the simulated reality that is the Matrix. They are now in a position to free other minds looking for the truth. Neo's inquisitive hacking brings him to Morpheus' attention. Inside the Matrix, he gives Neo a pill that will enable the rebels to locate his body in the real world, where it is operating as an energy source for the ruling machines. Neo's mind is released from the Matrix as the connection to his brain is severed and the cables that drain off his energy are ripped away. He emerges from the amniotic-like fluid of his prison cell gasping for breath and is taken on board the Nebuchadnezzar by the rebels where he is confronted with a less than desirable reality.

Once freed, Neo has to relearn the basic nature of his existence. Life on the ship is far from comfortable — he has exchanged material satisfaction for the knowledge of reality. This is a difficult transition for Neo. Morpheus explains: 'We never free a mind once it's reached a certain age. It's dangerous, the mind has trouble letting go.'

Neo is determined to be in control of his life yet is willing to submit to the authority of his leader, Morpheus. Cypher, on the other hand, does not relish the freedom Morpheus has given him and confides in Neo that he wishes to go back to the Matrix.

Key Issue: Freedom

Freedom — a wonderfully evocative word describing a concept that we all react positively to. The world longs for many sorts of freedom, and Christians are no exception. Don't we all want freedom from terrors such as war, poverty, illness, disaster, pain, suffering? We don't want oppression, we want the freedom to enjoy life to the full, and to make the most of the world we live in. We want people to be free, and countries to be free. The Matrix explores the idea of a world which is not free in any sense, and where its inhabitants do not even know it. Neo has some hard choices to make before he can experience freedom. His freedom in part means recognising the truth of the set-up. Is our world in a similar position? What does freedom mean for twenty-first century humanity? What does the Bible say about freedom, and is it relevant? What is true freedom?

Bible Study

For this study we have based all the questions on just two passages from the Bible — John 8:31–59 and Romans 6. You might like to stick to one of these right through your study. If you do, it would be a good idea to read the whole passage at the start.

Choose one question from each section.

1. Slavery

You are a slave, Neo. Like everyone else you were born into bondage, born into a prison that you cannot smell or taste or touch — a prison for your mind.
(Morpheus)

◆　Read John 8:31–41. What did Jesus think his hearers needed freeing from? Why didn't they see their need for freedom?

Leaders: Jesus' hearers claimed that they had never been slaves — they evidently thought that he was talking about political freedom (from the Romans). Jesus makes it clear that he is talking about spiritual freedom (v. 34). Central to understanding this passage is an idea of sonship which was important in their culture (and still is in many rural parts of the world today) — a son does what his father does. So, a fisherman's son becomes a fisherman, etc. Jesus uses this idea to tell his hearers that they don't act like the one they claim as their father (Abraham) so they are not his children. Instead, they do what Satan does and what they have heard from him, so demonstrating that they are his children.

◆　Read Romans 6:16–23. What does it mean to be a slave to sin? What are the consequences of being a slave to sin?

2. Choice

I'm trying to free your mind, Neo, but I can only show you the door. You're the one that has to walk through it. You have to let it all go, Neo — fear, doubt and disbelief. Free — your — mind. (Morpheus)

♦ Read John 8:37–47. What choice did the people have to make? How does this choice show itself in our actions?

Leaders: See note above.

♦ Read Romans 6:8–14. What does it mean to 'die with Christ'? *How* do we count ourselves dead to sin?

3. True Freedom

As long as the Matrix exists, the human race will never be free. (Morpheus)

♦ Read John 8:31–36. What does Jesus say true freedom is? How do we experience it?

Leaders: Holding to Jesus' teaching — persevering with it — marks people out as genuinely being his disciples. This leads them to an experience of Jesus as the truth, which liberates them (v. 32). Knowing the truth is not simply a question of understanding it but being committed to living it. Jesus — as the unique Son of God — sets people free from slavery to sin and its consequences (v. 35–36).

♦ Read Romans 6:1–18. What have we been freed from? What is true freedom?

Leaders: Paul is clear that we have been freed from sin. Yet sin is still very much part of our lives — as Paul recognises in Romans 7:14–25. We have been delivered from sin but we still need Christ to deliver us from our 'bodies of death' (7:24). The ultimate realisation of our freedom is in the new heavens and the new earth. Meanwhile, we live in the overlap — free from slavery to sin but not yet fully free from sin dragging us down. Paul explores this tension in Romans 7.

4. Consequences

Free — you call this free? All I do is what he tells me to do! (Cypher)

Leaders: Neither Jesus nor Paul see freedom from slavery to sin as a life without constraints. Jesus says that those who are free are his disciples and we demonstrate the reality of this by persevering with his teaching (John 8:31–32) — i.e. believing it and obeying it. If people are slaves to sin, they do the things that their father, the Devil, does. By implication, if we have been freed from slavery to sin, we have become sons of God and we should be like our Father (see leaders' notes under section 1 above). Paul says the same thing by contrasting slavery to sin with slavery to righteousness (Romans 6:16–18). We must be slaves to one or the other. It is important to remember, however, that we are not freed from slavery to sin because we are obedient to God. Rather, we want to be obedient to God because we have been freed from slavery to sin. It is a mark of our gratitude and a demonstration of God's grace at work in us.

♦ Read John 8:31–47. Jesus as the Son of God is ultimately free. Does this mean he does as he pleases? How does the relationship between freedom and obedience work for us?

♦ True freedom brings consequences. According to the whole of Romans 6, what does Paul say these are? What verses would you use to support your conclusions?

Implications

You have to understand, most of these people are not ready to be unplugged. And many of them are so inert, so hopelessly dependent on the system that they will fight to protect it. (Morpheus)

Choose one or more questions.

♦ How do we walk the path of Jesus' freedom, rather than just understand it?

♦ What does true freedom mean for you?

♦ Jesus promises us the truth. The truth is not always what we want to hear. How, then, can it lead us to freedom?

♦ How would you describe the benefits of the freedom Jesus offers to someone who had not experienced it yet? What do you think would be the most appealing aspect?

♦ How realistic is it to work for political, social or personal freedom in a fallen world?

♦ Does freedom mean being without constraints? In what ways do constraints upon us liberate us rather than limit us?

Prayer

Spend some time praying through these issues.

Background Reading

You will find links to some background reading on the Connect Bible Studies website: www.connectbiblestudies.com/uk/catalogue/0002/background.htm

Discuss

Discuss this study in the online discussion forums at www.connectbiblestudies.com/discuss

Members' sheet: The Matrix — Part 3

Summary

Morpheus is captain of the Nebuchadnezzar, a hovercraft crewed by rebels who have been freed from the simulated reality that is the Matrix. They are now in a position to free other minds looking for the truth. Neo's inquisitive hacking brings him to Morpheus's attention. Inside the Matrix, he gives Neo a pill that will enable the rebels to locate his body in the real world, where it is operating as an energy source for the ruling machines. Neo's mind is released from the Matrix as the connection to his brain is severed and the cables that drain off his energy are ripped away. He emerges from the amniotic-like fluid of his prison cell gasping for breath and is taken on board the Nebuchadnezzar by the rebels where he is confronted with a less than desirable reality.

Once freed, Neo has to relearn the basic nature of his existence. Life on the ship is far from comfortable — he has exchanged material satisfaction for the knowledge of reality. This is a difficult transition for Neo. Morpheus explains: 'We never free a mind once it's reached a certain age. It's dangerous, the mind has trouble letting go.'

Neo is determined to be in control of his life yet is willing to submit to the authority of his leader, Morpheus. Cypher, on the other hand, does not relish the freedom Morpheus has given him and confides in Neo that he wishes to go back to the Matrix.

Key Issue

Bible Study notes

Implications

Prayer

The Matrix

Andy & Larry Wachowski
(Warner, 1999)

Part Four: Faith

Neo, sooner or later you're going to realise, just as I did, there's a difference between knowing the path and walking the path.
(Morpheus)

Please read Using Connect Bible Studies *before leading a Bible study using this material.*

Opening Questions

Choose one of these questions.

How have you exercised faith in other people today?	'It doesn't matter what you put your faith in as long as you are sincere.' Do you agree?
Did you test your seat for faults before you sat down? Why not?	Is it possible to live without any faith in anything or anyone?

Summary

Morpheus has been searching the Matrix for years. The Oracle told him that he would find the one who would set the human race free from the machines. Her words fuelled his belief in the One and gave him the faith to search. Morpheus knows that his search is over when he rescues Neo from the Matrix: 'You are the One, Neo. You see, you may have spent the last few years looking for me, but I have spent my entire life looking for you.'

Neo himself is far from believing that he is the One. When Morpheus takes him to visit the Oracle, she confirms his doubt: 'Being the One is just like being in love. No one can tell you you're in love, you just know it.' She also tells him that a day will come when he will have to choose between saving his own life and saving Morpheus's.

Cypher betrays Morpheus in return for a life of luxury back inside the Matrix. Morpheus allows the Agents to capture him so that Neo can escape. The prophecy Neo received comes true: 'Morpheus believed something and he was ready to give his life for what he believed. I understand that now. But that's why I have to go ... Because I believe in something ... I believe I can bring him back.' As Neo prepares to sacrifice himself, his faith grows and he finds that he is the One after all.

Key Issue: Faith

Faith is an important theme in the Matrix. Morpheus is motivated by faith, both in his search for Neo and in his belief in him once he had found him. Neo has to exercise faith in his new companions in order to discover the truth of the world he is trapped in. He then has to work out whether to have faith in their belief that he is 'the One'. Only faith in this idea will help him to overcome his enemies. So what is faith? Do we all have it, and how does if affect us? Can we, like Neo, believe in ourselves? Christians argue that the object of our faith is of pivotal importance, but what does that mean in practice? What happens when faith is tried and tested?

Bible Study

Choose one question from each section.

1. Faith in self

If Morpheus was right, then there's no way I can pull this plug. I mean if Neo's the One, then there'd have to be some kind of a miracle to stop me. Right? I mean how can he be the One if he's dead? (Cypher)

Leaders: Having killed Tank back on the ship, Cypher is convinced that he can kill Neo who is stuck in the Matrix with Trinity. Just as he prepares to pull out Neo's lifeline, Tank summons up the strength to stop him. Cypher's belief in himself and lack of faith in Neo cannot change the fact that Neo is the One.

◆   Read Daniel 4:29–37. Why did these events happen to Nebuchadnezzar? How does Nebuchadnezzar change his perceptions of himself?

   Leaders: Nebuchadnezzar's self-belief cannot alter the reality that God is sovereign.

◆   Read Psalm 49. What are the consequences of having faith in ourselves and our own resources? What do you think the Psalmist means by 'understanding' in verse 20?

2. Faith in God

After he died, the Oracle prophesied his return and that his coming would hail the destruction of the Matrix, end the war, bring freedom to our people. That is why there are those of us who have spent our entire lives searching the Matrix, looking for him. I did what I did because I believe that search is over.
(Morpheus)

◆   Read Isaiah 26:1–15. What does Isaiah say God is like? What are the characteristics of those who have faith in him? How does it affect their actions and perspectives?

   Leaders: This passage contrasts well with the Daniel passage above.

♦ Luke 7:1–10. What was so amazing about the centurion's faith? What do we learn about how Jesus responds to a person's faith?

Leaders: Note that this Roman centurion had not seen Jesus, only heard of him.

3. Lack of faith

I know what you're thinking — 'cause right now I'm thinking the same thing. Actually, I've been thinking it ever since I got here — why, oh why, didn't I take the blue pill? (Cypher)

Leaders: Even though Cypher initially had enough faith to take the red pill, once he knew the full implications of the truth he longed to return to his comfortable old life, where 'ignorance is bliss'. He was prepared to exchange truth for a lie.

♦ Read Jeremiah 2:1–19. What happened to the Israelites' relationship with God? How did this affect them?

♦ Read Luke 8:22–25. What did the disciples put their faith in? Why didn't they have faith in Jesus?

Leaders: The disciples had to ask, 'Who is this?' It is a true understanding of who Jesus is that leads us to faith in what he can do.

4. Faith under fire

You're going to have to make a choice. In the one hand you'll have Morpheus' life and in the other hand you'll have your own. One of you is going to die. Which one will be up to you. (The Oracle)

Leaders: It is not until Neo has to make this difficult decision that he finally discovers his faith and starts to believe that he is the One. His faith is then rewarded when he sacrifices his life to save Morpheus but is resurrected with a greater belief and power.

♦ Read Psalm 37:1–11. What are faithful responses in times of testing? What difference do they make?

♦ Read James 1:1–12 and 1 Peter 1:3–9. Why does God test our faith? What do we gain from having our faith tested?

See also: Romans 6:22; Hebrews 12:7–11.

Implications

Neo, sooner or later you're going to realise, just as I did, there's a difference between knowing the path and walking the path. *(Morpheus)*

Choose one or more of the following questions.

- How can we encourage one another to be more faith-full?

- What areas of faith do you find difficult?

- How should we deal with the reality of seeing faithless people prosper?

- Should we, like Neo, ever have faith in ourselves?

- Can people see that you have faith in God?

- What would you say to someone who said, 'I wish I had your faith'?

Prayer

Spend some time praying through these issues.

You may also consider meditating on Isaiah 26.

Background Reading

You will find links to some background reading on the Connect Bible Studies website: www.connectbiblestudies.com/uk/catalogue/0002/background.htm

Discuss

Discuss this study in the online discussion forums at www.connectbiblestudies.com/discuss

Members' sheet: The Matrix — Part 4

Summary

Morpheus has been searching the Matrix for years. The Oracle told him that he would find the one who would set the human race free from the machines. Her words fuelled his belief in the One and gave him the faith to search. Morpheus knows that his search is over when he rescues Neo from the Matrix: 'You are the One, Neo. You see, you may have spent the last few years looking for me, but I have spent my entire life looking for you.'

Neo himself is far from believing that he is the One. When Morpheus takes him to visit the Oracle, she confirms his doubt: 'Being the One is just like being in love. No one can tell you you're in love, you just know it.' She also tells him that a day will come when he will have to choose between saving his own life and saving Morpheus's.

Cypher betrays Morpheus in return for a life of luxury back inside the Matrix. Morpheus allows the Agents to capture him so that Neo can escape. The prophecy Neo received comes true: 'Morpheus believed something and he was ready to give his life for what he believed. I understand that now. But that's why I have to go ... Because I believe in something ... I believe I can bring him back.' As Neo prepares to sacrifice himself, his faith grows and he finds that he is the One after all.

Key Issue

Bible Study notes

Implications

Prayer